To Johanna, Anne-Sophie, Matthias,
Tassilo and Arsène

CAPTIONS AND CREDITS

Cover and page 1
Jean-Baptiste Charpentier (1728-1806)
Marie-Antoinette, archduchess of Austria, future Dauphine of France 18th century. Oil on canvas. Ht. 64 cm, l. 52 cm.
Versailles, Musée national du château et de Trianon.
© Photo RMN/© Daniel Arnaudet

Page 2
Martin van Meytens the Younger (1695-1770)
The Emperor Francis I and the Empress Maria Theresa with their children on the terrace at Schönbrunn.
Ca. 1756. Oil on canvas. Ht. 200 cm, l. 182 cm.
Castle of Schönbrunn
© KHM, Vienna

Page 8
The Archduchess Marie Christine, daughter of Francis Ier and Maria Theresa (1742-1798)
The Imperial Family at home in Schönbrunn, on the morning of Saint Nicholas Day, 1762.
Gouache on paper. Ht. 30 cm, l. 45 cm.
Castle of Schönbrunn
© KHM, Vienna

Pages 16-17
Attributed to Georg Weikert (1745-1799)
Performance of the ballet "The Triumph of Love", detail
18th century. Oil on canvas. Ht. 2,88 m, l. 2,11 m
Versailles, Musée national du château et de Trianon.
© Photo RMN © Daniel Arnaudet/Gérard Blot.

Page 27
Martin van Meytens the Younger (1695-1760)
Portrait of the Archduchess Marie-Antoinette.
Ca. 1770. Oil on canvas. Ht. 91,5 cm, l. 73,5 cm.
Castle of Schönbrunn
© KHM, Vienna

Page 44
Page 44
François Dumont the Elder (1751-1831)
*Portrait of Marie-Antoinette and her children,*1790.
Miniature on ivory. Ht. 19,5 cm, l. 14,3 cm.
Paris, Musée du Louvre.
© Photo RMN/ © Michèle Bellot

Page 45
Hubert Robert (1733-1808)
View of the "Green Carpet" at Versailles, detail
18th century. Oil on canvas. Ht. 124 cm, l. 19 cm.
Versailles, Musée national du château et de Trianon.
© Photo RMN/© Droits réservés

PUBLISHED BY
Catherine de Duve, Kate'Art Editions
Pierre Vallaud,Réunion des musées nationaux
Catherine Marquet, Réunion des musées nationaux

COORDINATING EDITOR
Josette Grandazzi, Réunion des musées nationaux
Marie-Dominique de Teneuille, Réunion des musées nationaux

ART DIRECTION
Kate'Art Editions

TRANSLATED BY
Nathalie Trouveroy

ACKNOWLEDGMENTS:
The authors wish to thank Evelyne Lever, Christine Bourdeaux, Pierre Vallaud, Priscilla d'Oultremont,
Antoine de Spoelberch, Nathalie Trouveroy, Daniel de Duve, Benoît Sibille, Johanna, Gabrielle, Marie and Joséphine,
and all the people who participated in the making of this book.

www.happymuseum.com

Marie-Antoinette

Catherine de Duve and Thierry Bosquet

A historical tale

rmn

KATE'ART
EDITIONS

The Imperial Family. In the cradle, Marie-Antoinette.

The childhood of a Princess

Many, many years ago - over two hundred and fifty years - in the Hofburg palace in Vienna, there lived an empress and an emperor, Maria-Theresa and Francis I of Austria. They loved each other very much, and they had fourteen children already. One night, as dusk fell over the Imperial city, bells started ringing from every church tower, announcing good news: "A little princess is born, light as a feather." The baby was the fifteenth child of the empress. She was given the lovely name of Marie-Antoinette, and no one suspected what fate lay in store for her...

Four years later, little Antoine, as she is called in the family, celebrates the birthday of her beloved father, the emperor. She will sing in public for the first time, accompanied by her brothers and sisters. In Vienna, everybody simply loves music!

Marie-Antoinette is seven years old when a little boy, just the same age, arrives at the Palace in Schönbrunn. He is coming from Salzburg with his father and sister, and his name is Wolfgang Amadeus Mozart. When plays the clavichord, he sounds like an angel ! But as he bows to his audience, the little musician slips and falls headlong on the wooden floor… Wham ! Everyone laughs as he lies sprawling on the ground… Only Marie-Antoinette kindly helps him to get up, adjusting his clothes and his little parade sword.

"You, Mademoiselle, are much nicer than the others. When we both grow up, I shall marry you !" says little Mozart very seriously to the smiling Princess.

"Today's the big day!" Marie-Antoinette cries out as she wakes up.

"Get up, it's Saint Nicholas Day! He certainly came down the chimney last night to bring us gifts."

The children run all over the palace. "Where is he? Where is he? Which chimney did he climb down?" they wonder.

They race down the hallways, opening every door and slipping on the floor. Still nothing! Breathless, they finally reach the little yellow sitting room where the emperor, in his robe and nightcap, reads a letter by the fireside.

"What brings you here so early and in such good spirits?" their father asks with a smile.

There is a surprise for them…

"Look here!" cries Ferdinand, looking in awe at the carpet laden with gifts.

"Hurray!" shout the children.

Saint Nicholas has brought them candy, toys and money. Ferdinand finds a wooden soldier in his shoe, and Marie-Antoinette a lovely porcelain doll.

"How pretty she is!" exclaims the little princess, delighted. "Just the one I was hoping for!"

But what happened? Maximilian weeps bitter tears. The Saint's servant, who accompanies him to punish naughty children, left a bundle of prickly straw in his shoe. His elder sister Marie-Christine comforts him with a plateful of delicious heart-shaped cookies.

As every year, the Imperial family settles in the summer palace at Schönbrunn, a league away from Vienna. Marie-Antoinette strolls happily through the gardens, chasing the butterflies, counting the dots on the ladybugs and smelling the gorgeous roses.

The emperor has just received an unusual gift from the Sultan: a camel!

Little Antoine calls her brothers and sisters.

"Quick, let's go see what it looks like!"

– But where is it? Does it have one hump, or two… or three?" wonders Ferdinand.They all have a good laugh.

"The first one to see its hump wins!" quips Charlotte.

Marie-Antoinette has never seen a camel except in a picture book. She runs as fast as she can and looks for it all over the menagerie. Hush! The puma is taking a nap. Watch out for the rhinoceros! It looks ferocious…

"But what is this noise?" she wonders. Magnificent, multi-colored parrots are making a racket.

"Ah! There it is, it has two humps! cries Marie-Antoinette. I won!"

Tea is served in the small Chinese drawing room.

"Mmmhh… Delicious!" The table is laden with a scrumptious mountain of pastries, tiny multi-colored cakes and cream puffs.

"Be quiet! Don't let Mother catch us, she doesn't like us to eat sweets!" the children whisper.

$\mathcal{W}$inter has covered the land with a snowy carpet. All wrapped up in furs, the children race wildly to their sleigh. The cheerful team is all set to go. Maximilian gives the signal. But suddenly: "Watch out!" and whoosh! the sleigh turns over. They all roll down the hill, landing deep in the snow. "You have turned into snowmen!" laughs Marie-Antoinette, looking at her brothers and sisters, all white from top to toe. And they all giggle.

Back at the Palace, the children can't stop sneezing!

"Aaah-chooo"! sneezes Marie-Antoinette. "Aaah-CHEEE!" Charlotte follows.

The two sisters are inseparable. If one of them is ill, the other one is sure

to be. "Come on!" says the nanny. "In bed, both of you, with a hot water bottle

at your feet! What got into you, rolling in the snow like two fools? And look at

you now, what calamity!" The girls obey, chuckling behind her back.

*I*t's time for a dance and music class.

How graceful she looks! The little girl carries her head high and straight, with natural elegance. She really looks like a princess. Her clavichord teacher has arrived. His name is Gluck. Marie-Antoinette likes him a lot; he is very patient with her.

"All right, Mademoiselle, let's start again from C, right here" he tells his young pupil.

An important event is going to happen at the palace. Joseph, the eldest child – and the future Emperor – is getting married soon. What frenzy! Everything has to be ready in time. The children rehearse a ballet called "The Triumph of Love". Ferdinand and Marie-Antoinette are the shepherds, while Maximilian plays Cupid, the little angel of Love. Our charming little shepherdess can't wait to get on stage. "How should I dress for the show? I must be beautiful!" she muses.

The empress has a strong sense of duty.

"My daughters will be queens!"

Marie-Antoinette must prepare to become the next queen of France.

But at thirteen, the young archduchess can hardly read and write. And when she does, it is painfully slow, full of spelling mistakes and ink stains...

It is high time to perfect her education. She has so much to catch up with!

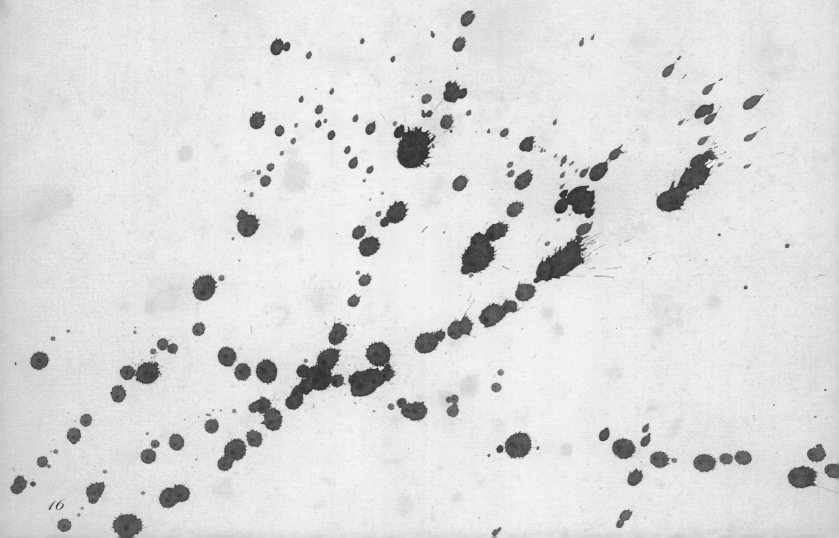

A Dauphine in Versailles

Marie-Antoinette's fate is sealed. She will marry the future king of France, the Dauphin, and she must join him in Versailles.

The time has come to say goodbye…

Before her departure, balls, banquets, fireworks and concerts are organized to honor the future Dauphine. One morning, the empress gives her beloved daughter a last hug, with tender words: "Goodbye, my dear child. There will be many miles between us." Marie-Antoinette is speechless with emotion. Bravely, she fights her tears and steps into the splendid gilt carriage sent by the king of France.

A long procession of fifty-seven carriages takes away the young girl, her little dog and a few friends, whom she will have to part with when she enters her new country, France.

"I must leave you, my dearest brothers and sisters, but my heart is yours to keep", whispers the princess, watching her home and her happy childhood fade away in the distance. At the border, she has to say goodbye once more, this time to her friends and her beloved pet.

"I cannot tell you how deeply your kindness touched me. Take good care of yourselves and of my dear little dog."

The marriage ceremony is concluded there, between France and the Austrian Empire, and Marie-Antoinette hasn't even seen the bridegroom yet. A royal envoy stood in for him. What a strange custom! "Where is my Prince?" the new dauphine wonders. She will meet him further on, in a forest where king Louis XV is expecting her impatiently, along with his daughters and his grandson: the dauphin Louis-Auguste, Marie-Antoinette's new husband.

When Marie-Antoinette arrives at the palace in Versailles, after a long, three-week journey, she discovers a weird crowd in powdered wigs, their white faces covered in rouge and tiny moles made of black silk.

"What strange hairdos they have here! And it looks like they dip their faces in a tub of flour! Why these two large red circles on their cheeks? Is this a masquerade or is it the fashion in Paris?" wonders the Dauphine.

Soon Marie-Antoinette discovers life at the French Court and its heavy "etiquette". There are rules for everything you do here! "Madame Etiquette", her stern lady-in-waiting, is always at her side to remind her of it. The princess is bored.

Her husband, Louis-Auguste, spends all his time hunting and she feels lonely.

*H*uge formal dinners are served in front of a crowd of onlookers. "This is ridiculous" she thinks. The Dauphine is losing her appetite. Everyone looks at her as if she were a strange animal in a zoo.

"Ah, it snows…" she sighs, remembering her happy childhood in Austria. But being homesick won't help. So she decides to have fun!

Sleigh-rides in the park, donkey rides and horse rides are followed by a night at the Opera, a play at the Comédie-Française or even better, a ball at the Opéra de Paris. There are also balls in Versailles, and Marie-Antoinette loves dancing. On Mondays the court dances at Madame la Dauphine's, and on Wednesdays at the Countess de Noailles', the tiresome "Madame Etiquette".

Days are passing by monotonously. Marie-Antoinette has to follow rules and customs set a hundred years earlier by the Sun-King Louis XIV, and she finds them terribly dull.

"Madame, it is traditional for the Court to watch you get up in the morning", Madame Etiquette declares with a frown.

"Is that so?" wonders Marie-Antoinette, surprised, "can't I get up and dress by myself?"

"Oh, your Highness, certainly not! These are the rules. When you wake up, you rise from your bed in the presence of the ladies. Then the Court is ushered in to watch you put on your make-up and wash your hands. After that, the Court retires and only the ladies stay." The countess has a little awkward cough. "Then your lady-in-waiting washes her hands before handing you your chemise. After that, your attendant hands you the dress, assisted by the

chief chambermaid and her helpers. But if a royal princess is present, the lady-in-waiting must defer to her and let her hand you the chemise. Does your Highness understand?"

"Blah blah blah… this is ridiculous!" Marie-Antoinette can't believe it. She thinks these customs are weird, not to mention very embarrassing.

"This is too much!" decides the Dauphine, without losing her good nature and graceful character. "From now on the morning rituals will be simplified: once her hair is brushed and her make-up done, the Dauphine will salute the court and retire to her chambers to get dressed." And she gets her way.

A Queen's entertainment

Four years have gone by. Marie-Antoinette is now the queen, and she has a passion for games. She plays backgammon or "cavagnol", a kind of bingo. Sometimes she plays for money, although the king has prohibited gambling because huge fortunes have been lost that way. But who can resist the young queen?

"What about a game of lansquenet or pharaoh?" she calls. "The king gave me permission to have one last game!"

The gambling went on for thirty-six hours! The court played non-stop till the morning of the next day. When the king heard about this endless game, the queen quipped: "Your Majesty allowed me one game, but did not specify how long it could be!" Her lovely smile would melt the toughest heart.

Laughing, the King replied: "Go on, you're naughty ruffians, all of you!"

The queen also loves horse races, a new fashion imported from England. But her favorite game is billiard, and she keeps a table in her private chambers, where she can retire away from the crowd.

Sometimes she enjoys the visit of her good friend, the painter Elisabeth Vigée-Lebrun.

"Try not move too much, your Majesty," says the artist, who is painting a portrait of the queen playing her harp. Marie-Antoinette smiles. She loves the company of her charming and talented friend.

The queen is also very busy redecorating the palace, selecting fabrics, furniture and novelties, and then there are new dresses and hairdos that need to be constantly reinvented. So many things to alleviate the boredom of life in Versailles! And why shouldn't she be the most elegant woman in France? Marie-Antoinette is brimming with ideas!

*I*n her sweet-scented yellow sitting room, Marie-Antoinette is chatting with her favorite hairdresser, Léonard.

"Let me crrreate for you a towerrring hairdo, as tall as my rrrespect for my Queen!" says the hairdresser, rolling his 'Rs. In order to give hair more volume, he crimps it up over a pouf. The artist gives his royal client a mask to protect her face while he powders her hair with starch to make it white.

"Oh, Monsieur" jokes the queen, "you look like a floured piece of fish, ready to be fried!"

Fixing those puffy cushions on top of the head is a complicated task!

"Ouch! Your pins hurt me, good Monsieur!"

"Parrrdon me, my Queen, I shall be morrre carrreful."

Léonard brings the final touch to the royal hair and adds translucent gauze, sublime feathers, ribbons and flowers…

"Your Majesty looks rrravishing!" says the "purveyor of capillary grace", holding a mirror for the queen.

Soon all the ladies at Court are flocking to Léonard's to get the most impressive puffed-up hairdos. They wear fantastic hats and extravagant headdresses with fancy names, like "ostrich-feather pouf" or "pageant of emotions pouf", as well as elaborate chignons from which roses cascade down.

Even current event like the American Independence are inspiring hairstyles. The "Belle-Poule" headdress recreates a frigate that won a famous battle at sea! How odd to see a full battleship perched on a lady's head...

"Phew… it's heavy!" mutter the ladies under their breath. Some of these fabrications are over three feet high, and the wearers end up looking like a wedding-cake or that new invention, a hot-air balloon… They can't even sit in their carriages anymore, and have to crouch between the seats.

Was there ever a sillier fashion? Where will it stop?

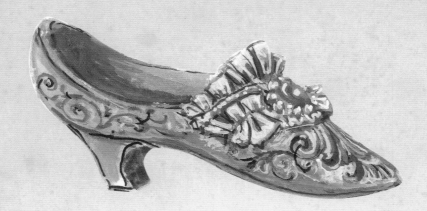

*B*ut what would you do if you had to spend your life moving from castle to castle, from party to party, subjected to the terrible boredom of etiquette and the cruelty of court gossip? What can you do when you're excluded from politics, from the problems of the kingdom, and that you have no children yet to love?

This may be why fashion has become Marie-Antoinette's main preoccupation. Every morning, the keeper of the wardrobe hands the first chambermaid a large book where swatches of fabric are pasted with sealing wax. The queen selects her outfits for the day by sticking a pin to each pattern: one for the morning dress, one for the informal afternoon dress, another for the full evening dress she'll wear at a card game or at supper.

The frivolous queen can't resist the gorgeous dresses, the sumptuous fabric and magnificent jewels that are constantly offered to her.

"What shall I choose? A pannier dress, the "impertinent pleasures" dress or the "love's cradle" one? What delightful creations!" she exclaims, looking at embroidered silks and fine laces.

The queen invents funny names for the latest fashionable colors: "flea stomach", "Dauphin's pooh"…

She wants her dressmaker, the formidable Mademoiselle Bertin, to create dresses that will make all other women swoon in envy.

"I'll have this one!" decides the queen. « It will be just perfect to dance at the Bal de l'Opéra!"

The extravagance of her two suppliers knows no bounds. Ribbons here, ostrich feathers there… The bills of Rose Bertin and Léonard are staggering. Marie-Antoinette's taste is terribly expensive.

"Who cares! I'll be serious later. Now let's have fun!" retorts the queen to those who would like her to be more careful.

*I*t is quite a feat to walk through the grand halls of Versailles, wearing those long, cumbersome court dresses, without stepping on another lady's hem. Do not lift your feet! You must glide elegantly on the polished floor of the majestic Galerie des Glaces. And if you don't know how to dance, watch your step… The queen has mastered this elegant art and all eyes are set on her gracious Majesty.

When the king and queen walk by, a mob of courtiers rushes to the scene. They all want to be seen and ask for favors, so they elbow their way to the front, hoping to get a single word from the sovereign. It's a real free-for-all, but what honor when after days or months, one finally gets a little royal nod! This is what court life is all about in Versailles…

Marie-Antoinette wants to get away from the formalities of the court. When her husband, king Louis XVI, is not away hunting, he spends hours in his locksmith's workshop, creating intricate mechanisms.

It's a real passion!

One day, the king gives his young wife a present beyond her wildest dreams.

"You love flowers, don't you" he says cheerfully. "Well, I have a bouquet for you!" and he gives her a sumptuous key, set with five hundred and thirty one diamonds…

"Oh! What a charming, delightful gift!" she exclaims, dazzled by the sparkle of this magnificent gift, glittering like countless tiny suns.

"This is the key to the Petit Trianon", he adds. Marie-Antoinette jumps for joy and kisses her blushing husband. Finally, she will have a real home, where she can be herself without being constantly watched by the whole court.

The renovation work begins "by the Queen's command". The garden is expensively redesigned. Hillocks, waterfalls, a large rock and even a small river are constructed! "Wouldn't it be charming to have a pretty little temple of Love, on an island full of roses?" No sooner said than done. An army of gardeners stands ready to fulfill the queen's every wish.

Inside, the Trianon is decorated in soft pastel hues: green, lilac, white, gold. Furniture and ornaments are inspired from the bucolic themes the queen likes so much: bird cages, flower baskets adorned with pretty ribbons.

This is Marie-Antoinette's own style, and it is exquisite!

Soon parties, shows and operas are organized there. On the stage of the small Trianon theatre, with its cardboard sets, Marie-Antoinette plays shepherdesses or servant girls with her "company of lords". Everyone claps enthusiastically when she appears. The queen seems to relive part of her happy childhood. After the show, all her guests are invited to share a fine supper.

"Let's eat and be merry!"

Marie-Antoinette tells her little group of select friends.

But this kind of privacy runs against the stately life of the court, and people begin to disapprove and resent her lack of attention. Tongues are wagging in Versailles!

"Have you ever seen such a thing? How dare she scorn the Court like that! Let's leave. Paris has become much more fun!" Little by little, the courtiers abandon the castle of Versailles, leaving Marie-Antoinette and her favorite companions by themselves.

*M*arie-Antoinette has finally become a mother, and it is her greatest joy. She brings up her children herself, with the help of a governess.

She still lives in the fantasy world she has created. She has built a charming hamlet, with a farm, a mill, a dairy and a lake… How romantic! The queen wants to live close to nature, and has taken to dressing in a very simple fashion, letting her hair hang freely on her shoulders. "A light muslin dress, a little scarf and a pretty straw hat are all I need" she muses.

arie-Antoinette loves to walk in her private gardens with her family, picking flowers, playing blind man's buff…

"Come on, children, let's go and fetch milk at the dairy farm!" The children laugh; they have so much fun riding in their little cart drawn by sheep.

But a storm is brewing… and they all run to the shelter of their home.

Soon History will catch up with them. But this is another story…